CONTENTS

A Hero Is Born

Aegeus, the king of Athens, watched as a great rock was rolled over where his sword and sandals lay. "When my son is strong enough to roll away this stone, send him to me," he said to Aethra, princess of Troezen. He was talking about Theseus, the unborn child that Aethra carried.

The Road to Athens

When Theseus was a teenager, he removed the the sword and sandals with ease and began his quest to reunite with his father. Rather than take the safer route by sea, Theseus struck out by road, a road that was infested with robbers. One by one, he defeated the worst of them and presented himself to the court of Aegeus.

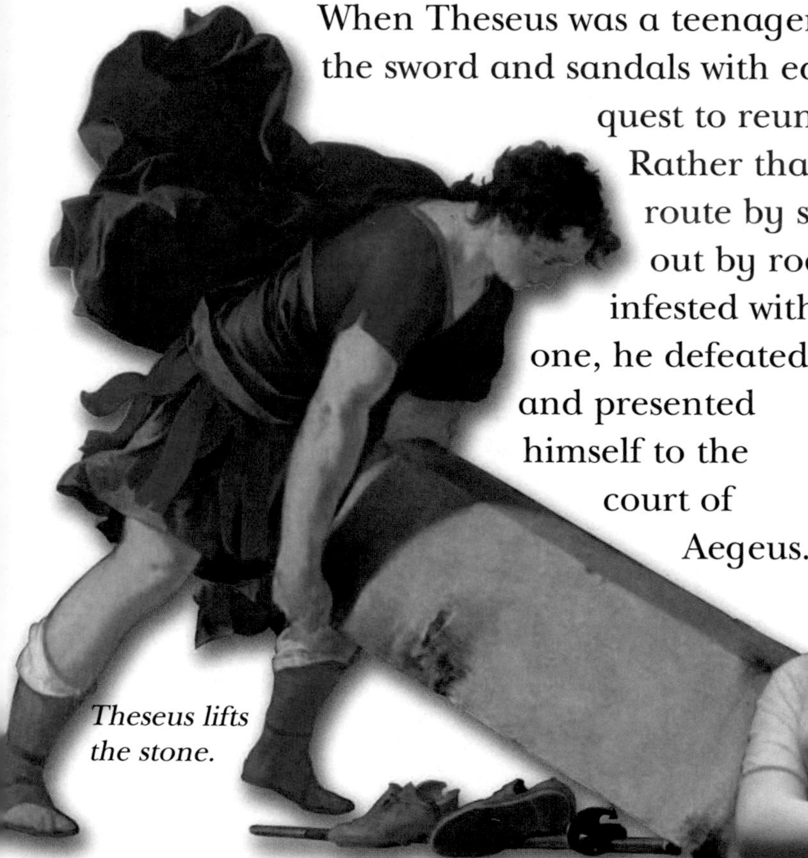

Theseus lifts the stone.

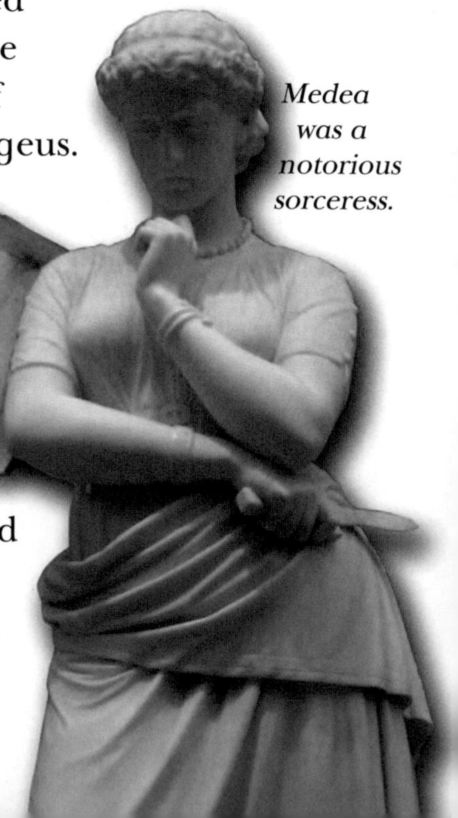

Medea was a notorious sorceress.

A Witch's Trap

Aegeus's new wife, Medea, grew alarmed when the boy introduced himself as the king's lost son. She filled Aegeus's mind with suspicion and persuaded him to poison Theseus with one of her potions.

GRAPHIC MYTHICAL HEROES

THESEUS
BATTLES THE MINOTAUR

BY GARY JEFFREY
ILLUSTRATED BY TERRY RILEY

Gareth Stevens
Publishing

Please visit our website, www.garethstevens.com.
For a free color catalog of all our high-quality books,
call toll free 1-800-542-2595 or fax 1-877-542-2596.

Library of Congress Cataloging-in-Publication Data

Jeffrey, Gary.
Theseus battles the Minotaur / Gary Jeffrey.
pages cm — (Graphic mythical heroes)
Includes index.
ISBN 978-1-4339-7528-8 (pbk.)
ISBN 978-1-4339-7529-5 (6-pack)
ISBN 978-1-4339-7527-1 (library binding)
1. Theseus (Greek mythology)—Juvenile literature. 2. Minotaur (Greek
mythology)—Juvenile literature. I. Title.
BL820.T5J44 2012
398.20938'02—dc23
                                                2012000225

First Edition

Published in 2013 by
Gareth Stevens Publishing
111 East 14th Street, Suite 349
New York, NY 10003

Designed by David West Books

Photo credits:
p4, Postdlf; p5bl, sailko, p5br, Marsyas;
p22t, A Gude, p22b, bitmask

Printed in China

CPSIA compliance information: Batch #DWS12GS: For further information contact Gareth Stevens, New York, New York at 1-800-542-2595.

A Close Call

As Theseus brought the poisoned wine cup to his lips, Aegeus suddenly recognized the shining hilt of the boy's sword. "No!" he shouted, and dashed the cup to the floor. "You are my son after all!" Medea fled, and Theseus was anointed heir to the kingdom.

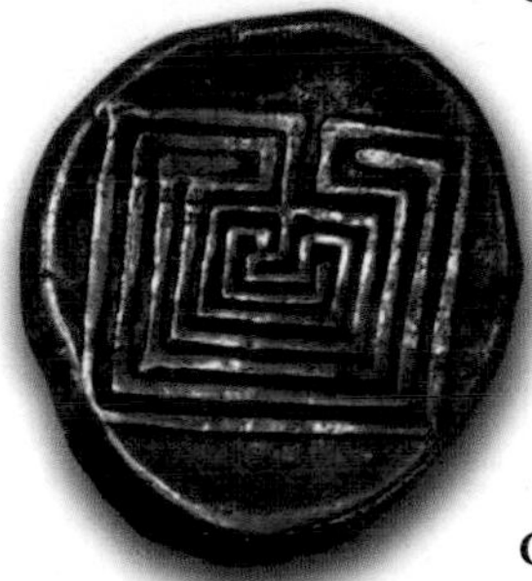

An ancient coin decorated with a labyrinth

A Deadly Debt

At that time, Athens was under a cloud of sadness. The son of King Minos of Crete had died under Aegeus's protection. Every year, seven youths and seven maidens were forced to travel to Crete to be fed alive to a monster called the Minotaur, which was kept in a labyrinth beneath Minos's palace. Eager to prove himself a hero, Theseus determined to go with the next group and face the Minotaur himself...

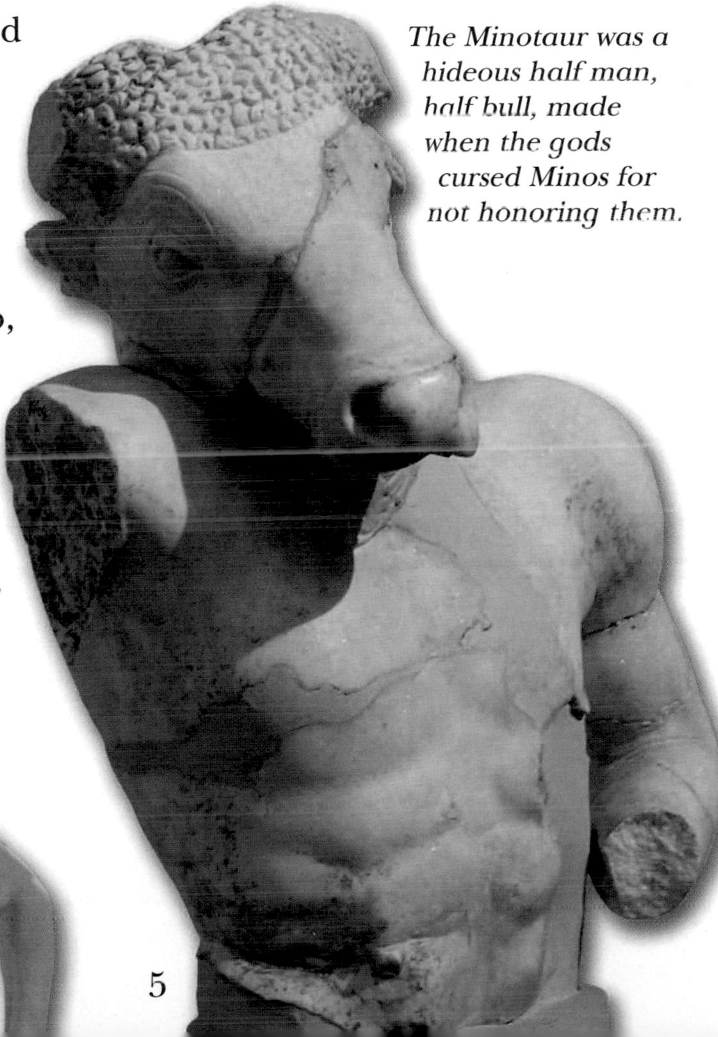

The Minotaur was a hideous half man, half bull, made when the gods cursed Minos for not honoring them.

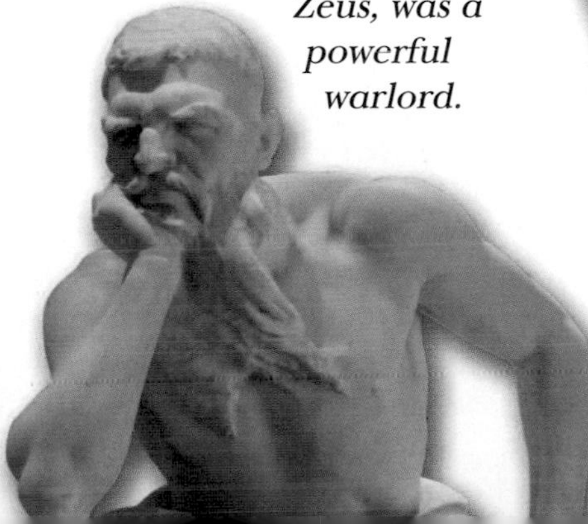

King Minos, a son of the god Zeus, was a powerful warlord.

Theseus Battles the Minotaur

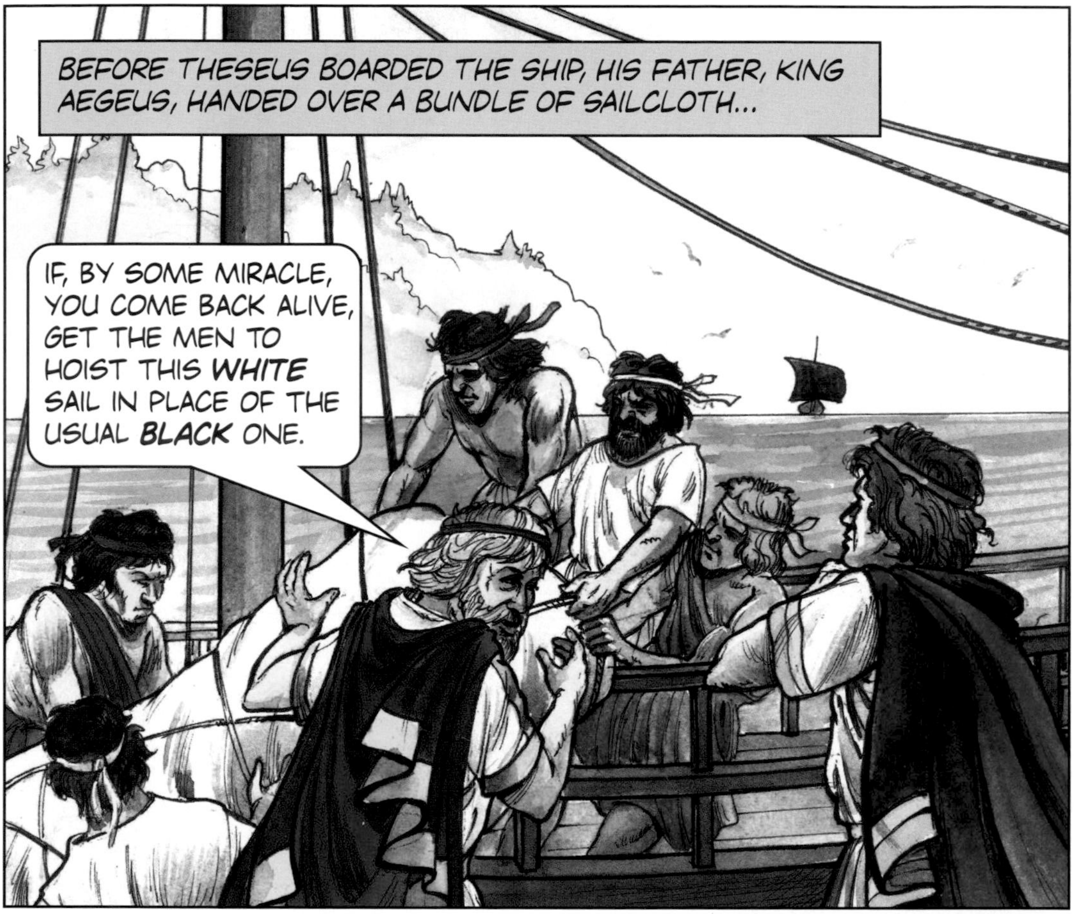
BEFORE THESEUS BOARDED THE SHIP, HIS FATHER, KING AEGEUS, HANDED OVER A BUNDLE OF SAILCLOTH...
IF, BY SOME MIRACLE, YOU COME BACK ALIVE, GET THE MEN TO HOIST THIS **WHITE** SAIL IN PLACE OF THE USUAL **BLACK** ONE.

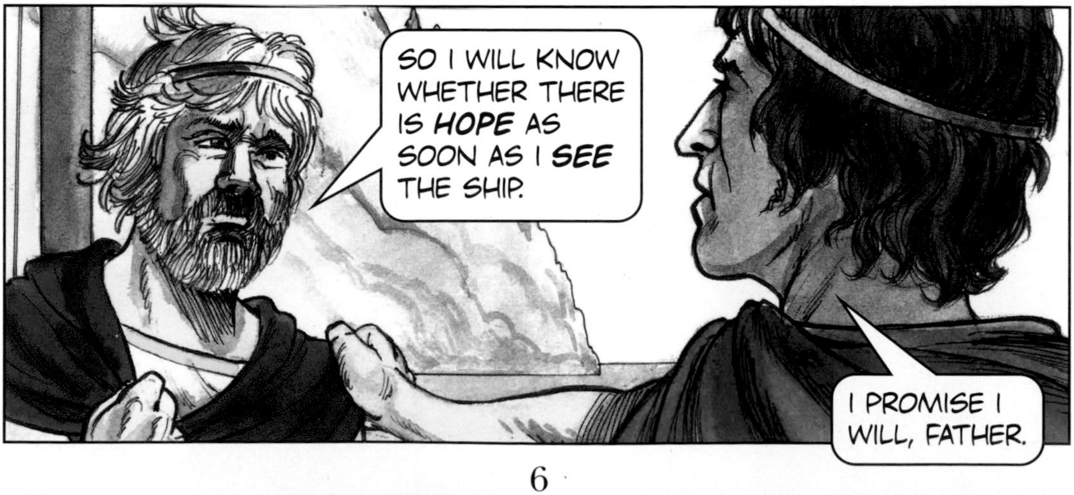
SO I WILL KNOW WHETHER THERE IS **HOPE** AS SOON AS I **SEE** THE SHIP.
I PROMISE I WILL, FATHER.

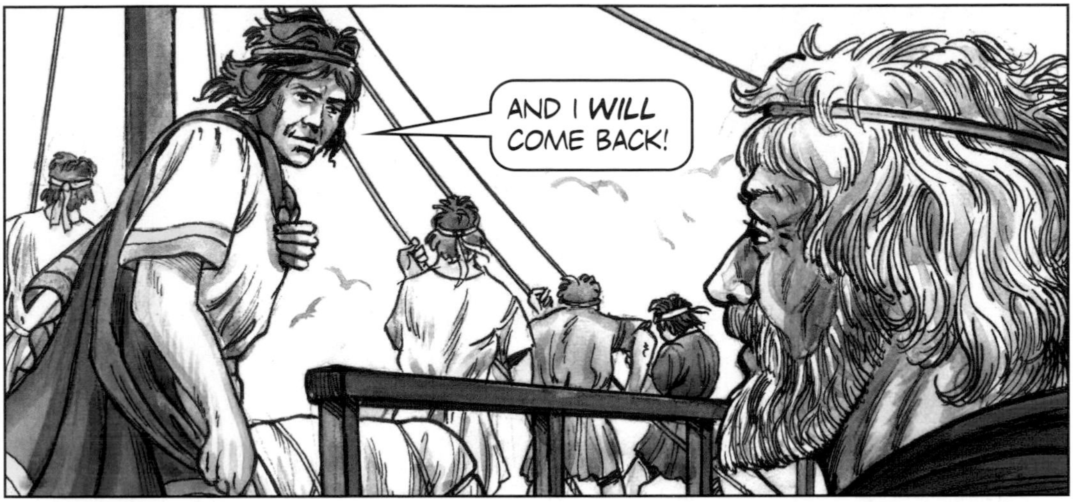
AND I **WILL** COME BACK!

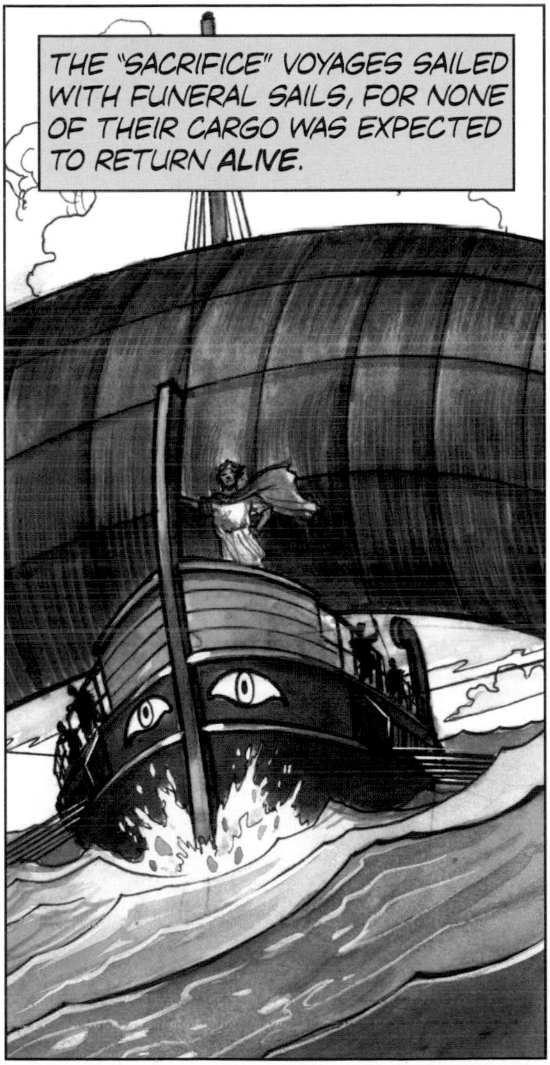
THE "SACRIFICE" VOYAGES SAILED WITH FUNERAL SAILS, FOR NONE OF THEIR CARGO WAS EXPECTED TO RETURN **ALIVE**.

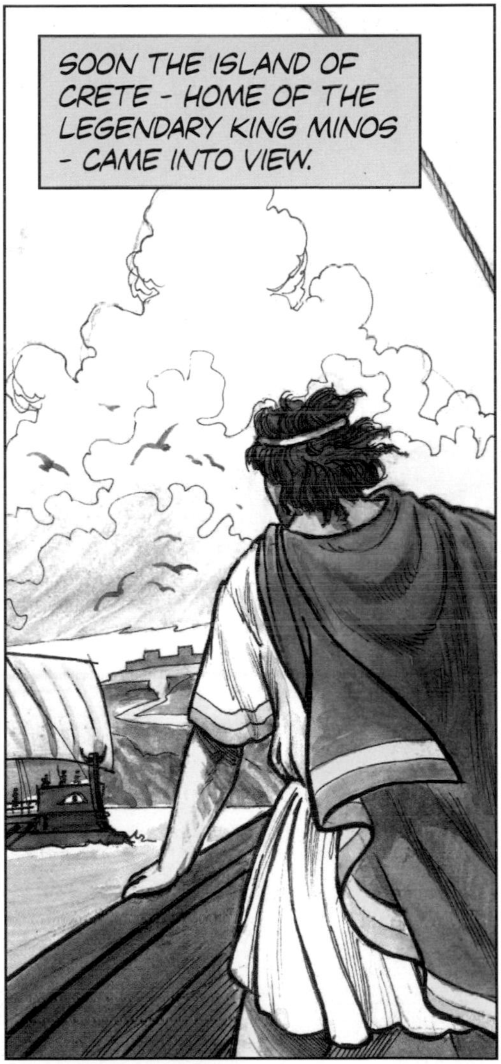
SOON THE ISLAND OF CRETE - HOME OF THE LEGENDARY KING MINOS - CAME INTO VIEW.

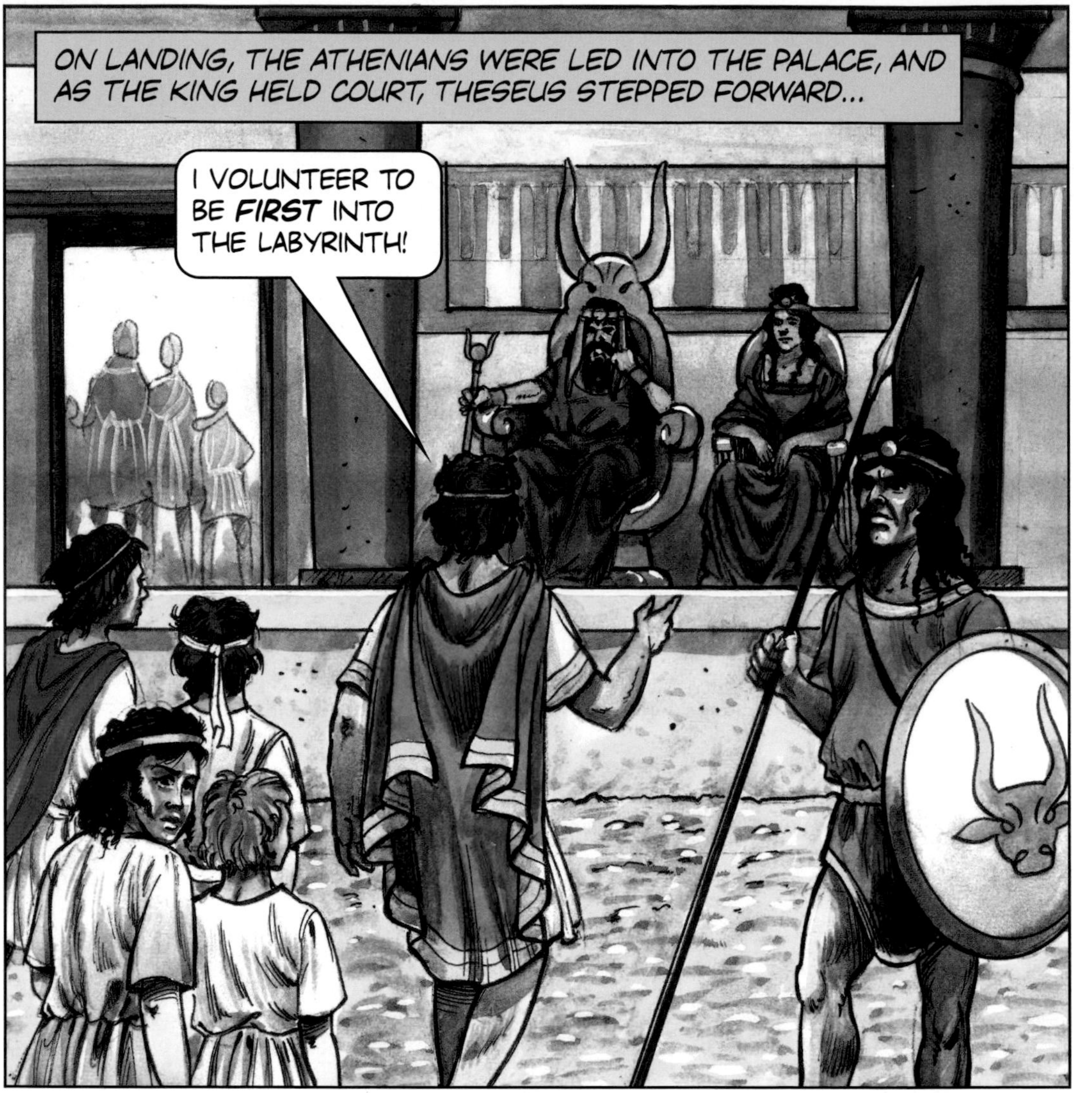
ON LANDING, THE ATHENIANS WERE LED INTO THE PALACE, AND AS THE KING HELD COURT, THESEUS STEPPED FORWARD...
I VOLUNTEER TO BE **FIRST** INTO THE LABYRINTH!

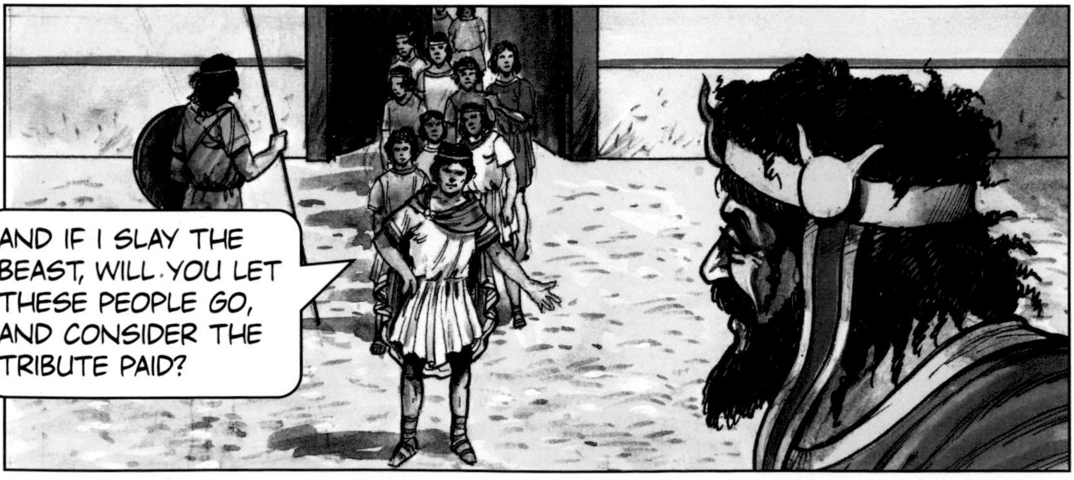
AND IF I SLAY THE BEAST, WILL YOU LET THESE PEOPLE GO, AND CONSIDER THE TRIBUTE PAID?

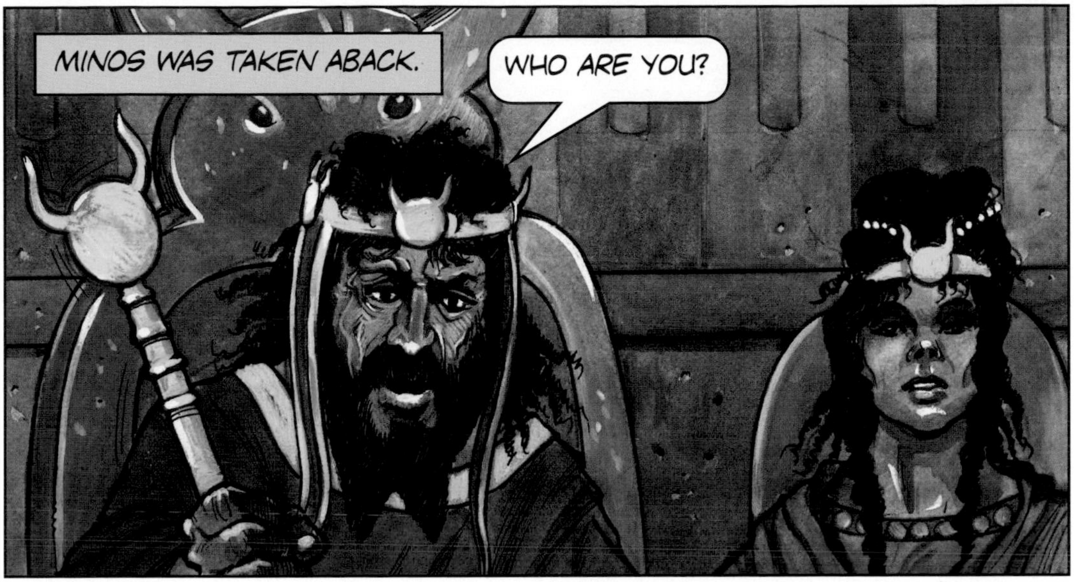
MINOS WAS TAKEN ABACK.
WHO ARE YOU?

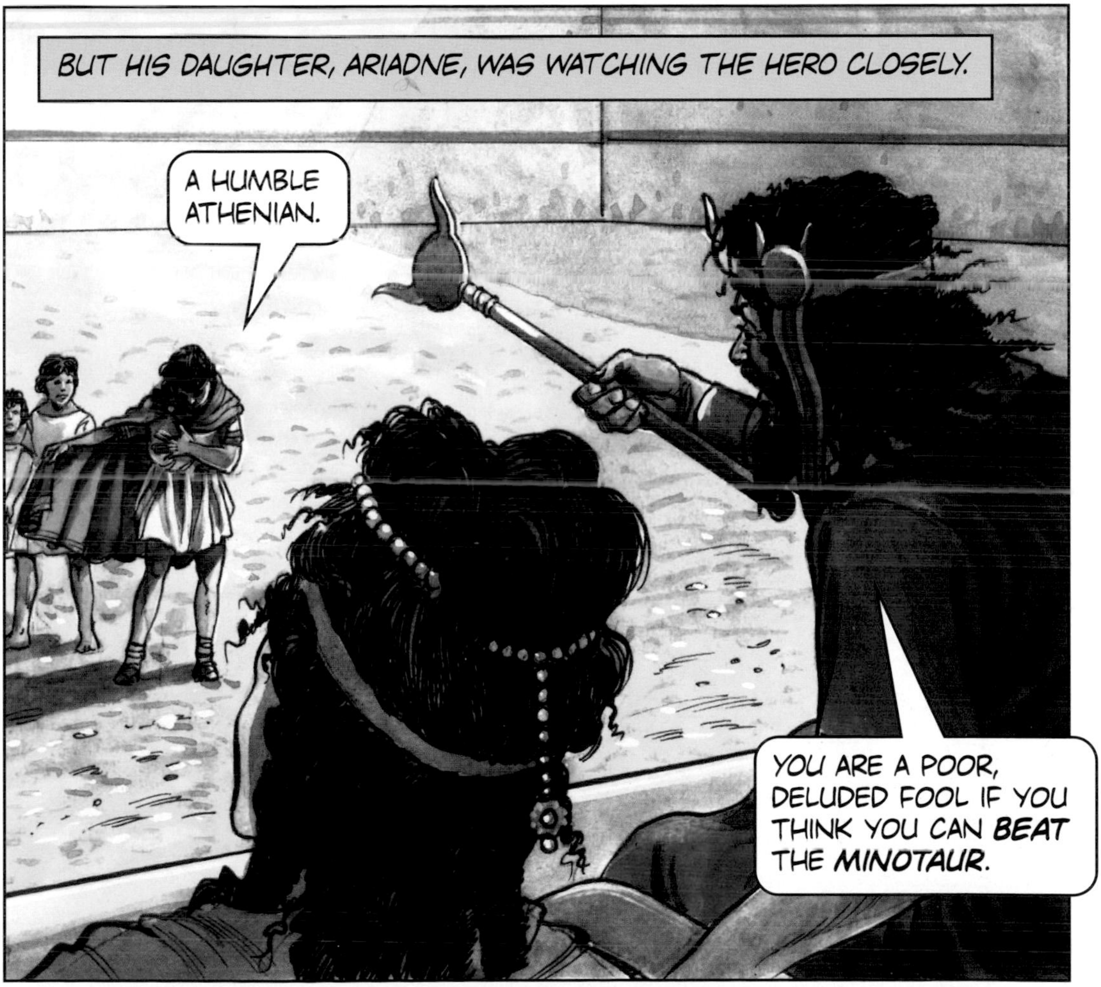
BUT HIS DAUGHTER, ARIADNE, WAS WATCHING THE HERO CLOSELY.
A HUMBLE ATHENIAN.
YOU ARE A POOR, DELUDED FOOL IF YOU THINK YOU CAN BEAT THE MINOTAUR.

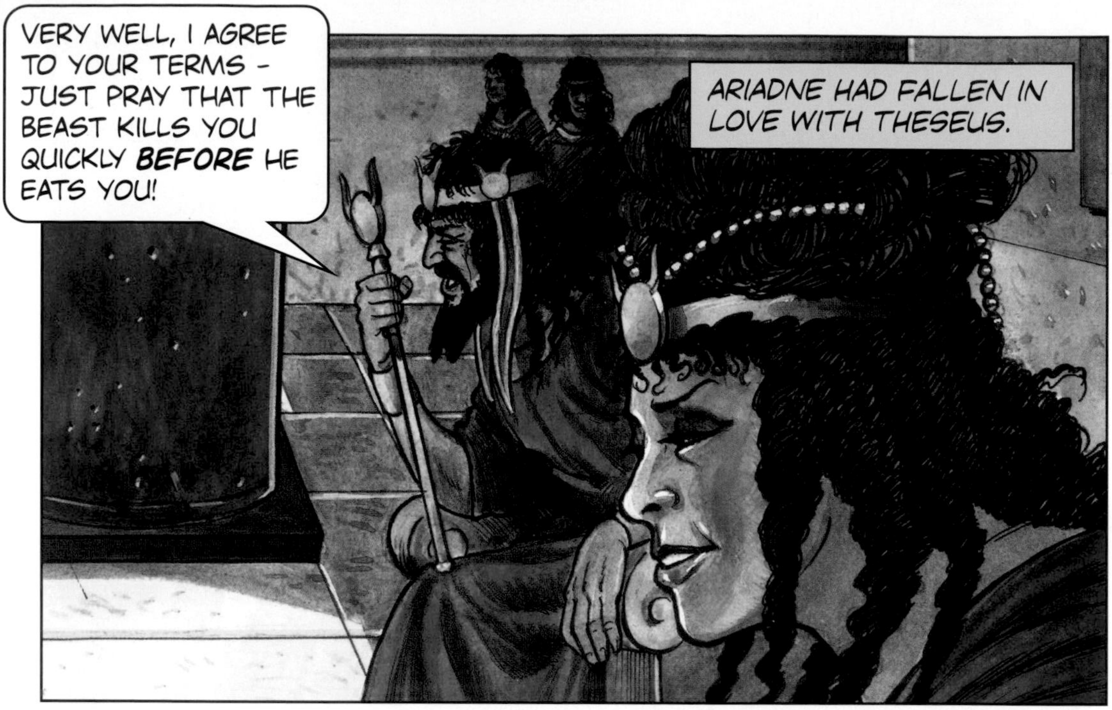
VERY WELL, I AGREE TO YOUR TERMS - JUST PRAY THAT THE BEAST KILLS YOU QUICKLY **BEFORE** HE EATS YOU!
ARIADNE HAD FALLEN IN LOVE WITH THESEUS.

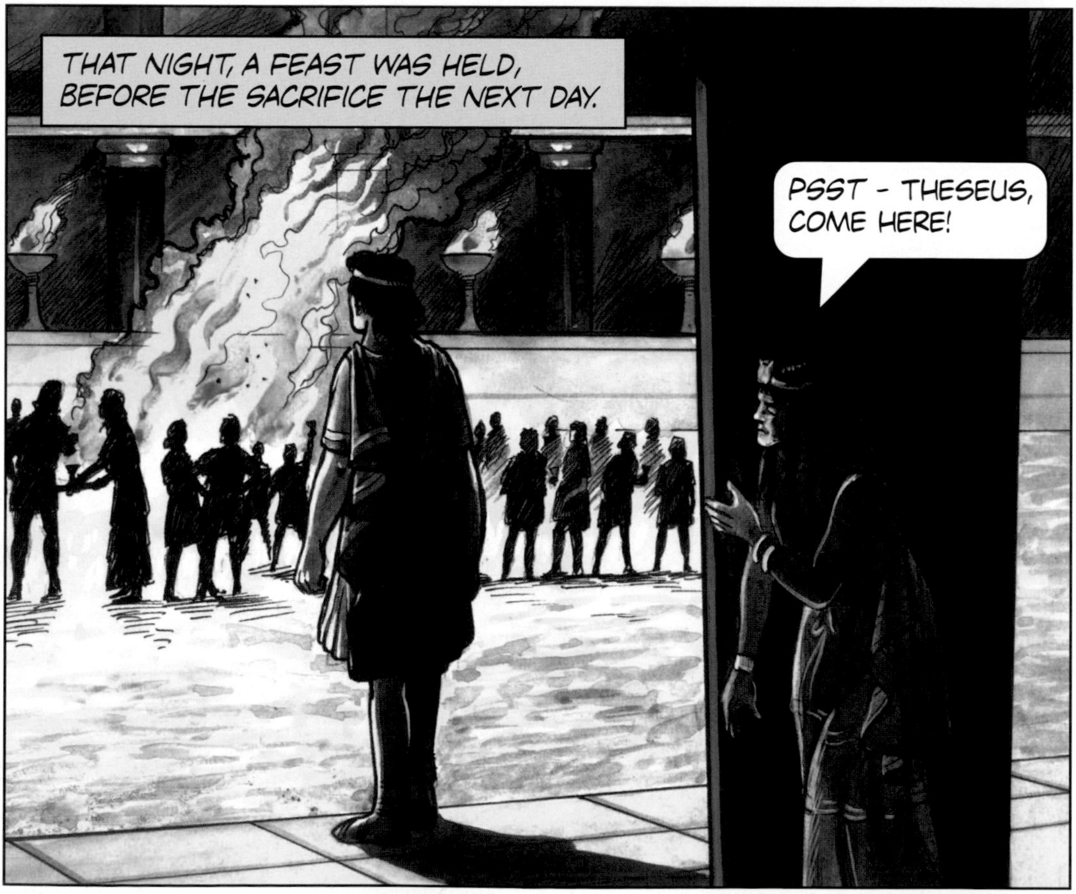
THAT NIGHT, A FEAST WAS HELD, BEFORE THE SACRIFICE THE NEXT DAY.
PSST - THESEUS, COME HERE!

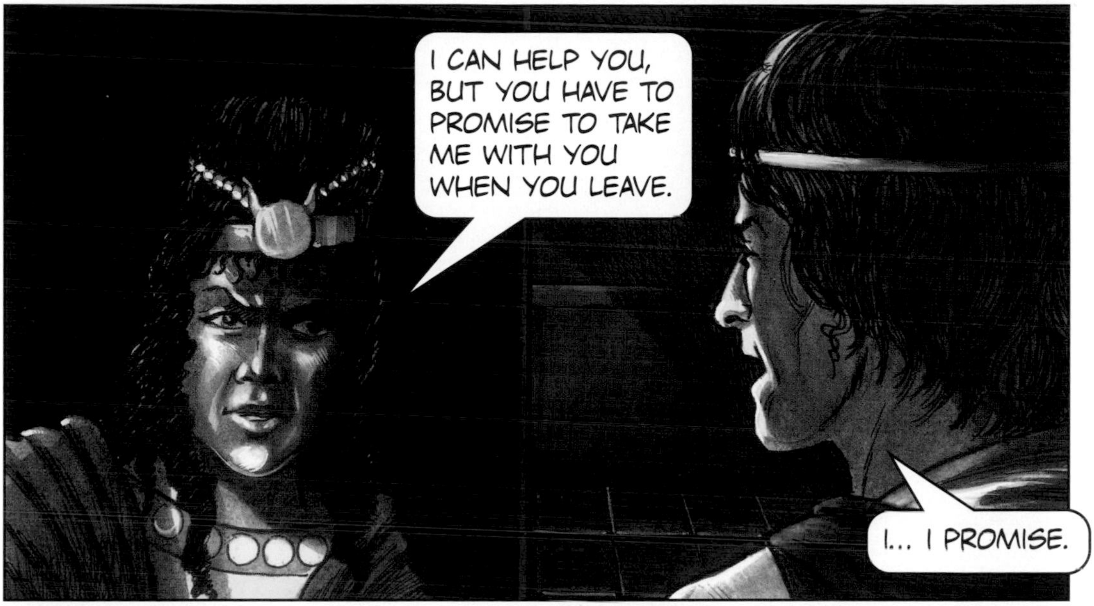
I CAN HELP YOU, BUT YOU HAVE TO PROMISE TO TAKE ME WITH YOU WHEN YOU LEAVE.
I... I PROMISE.

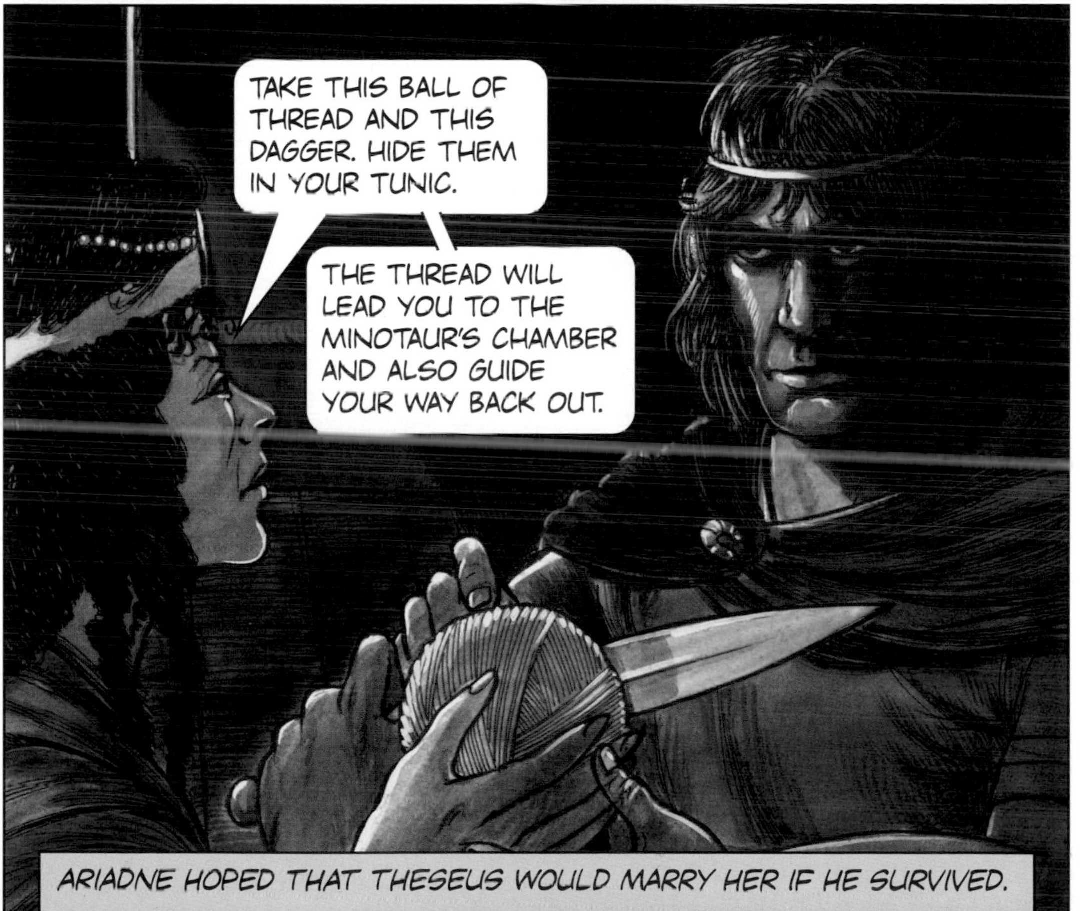
TAKE THIS BALL OF THREAD AND THIS DAGGER. HIDE THEM IN YOUR TUNIC.
THE THREAD WILL LEAD YOU TO THE MINOTAUR'S CHAMBER AND ALSO GUIDE YOUR WAY BACK OUT.
ARIADNE HOPED THAT THESEUS WOULD MARRY HER IF HE SURVIVED.

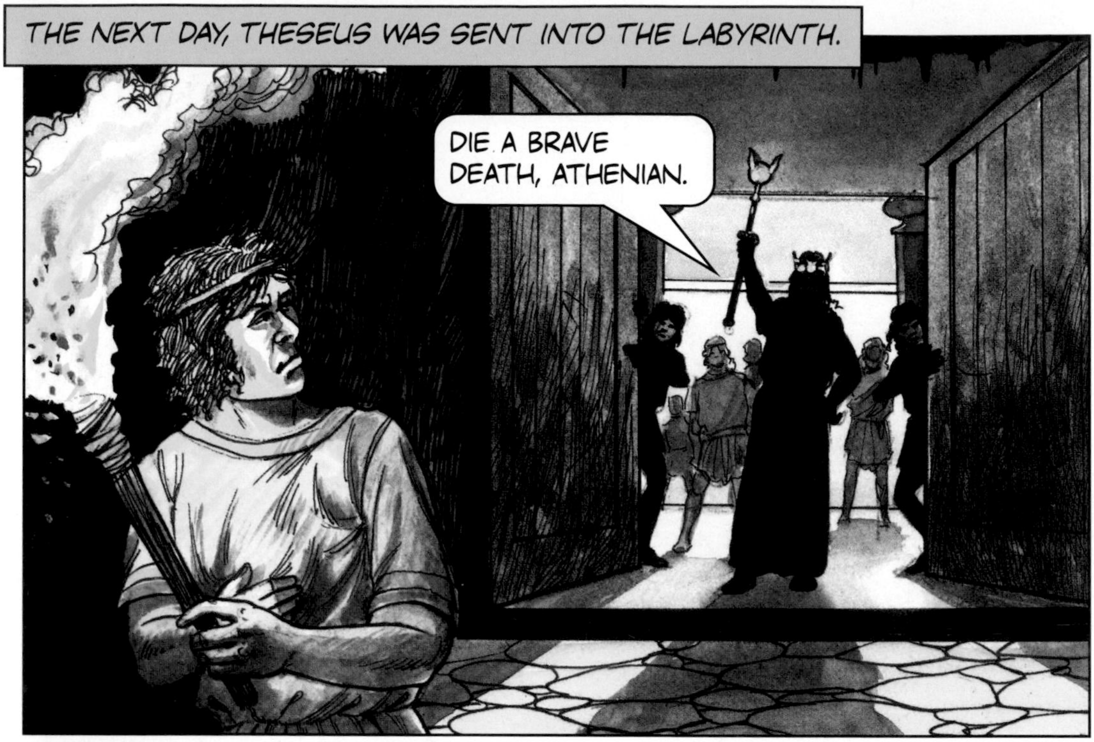
THE NEXT DAY, THESEUS WAS SENT INTO THE LABYRINTH.
DIE A BRAVE DEATH, ATHENIAN.

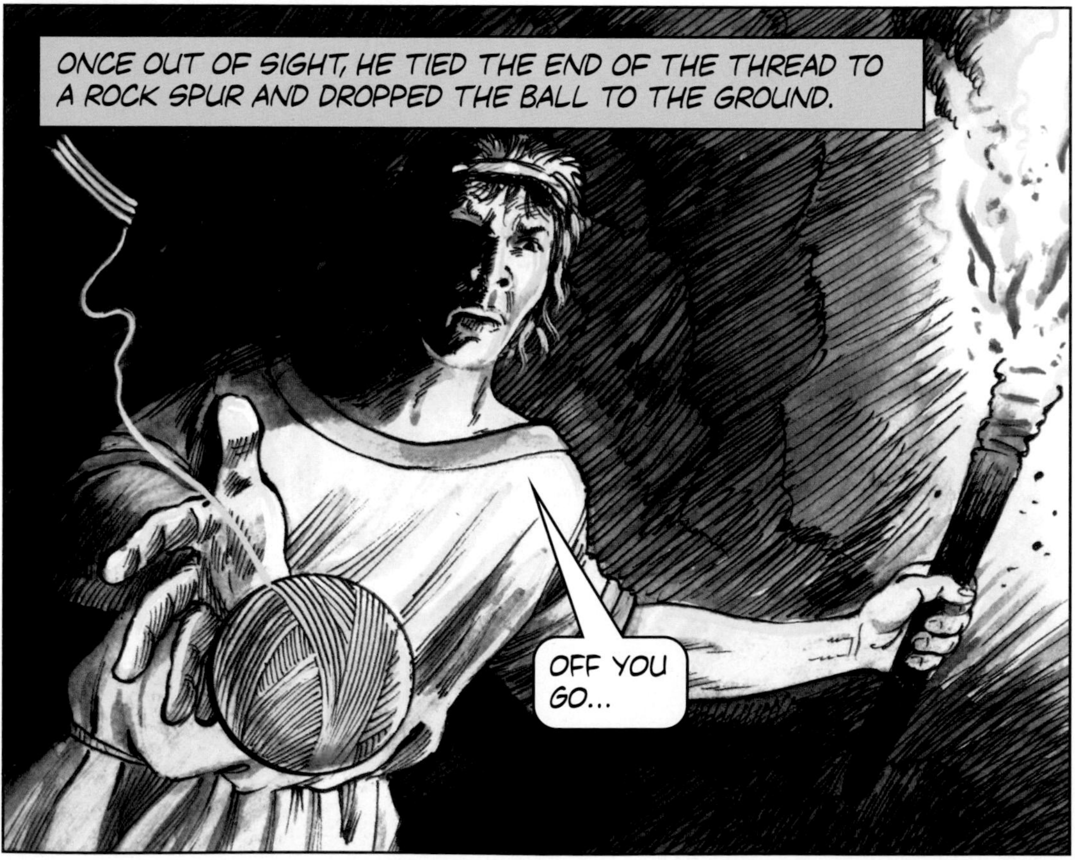
ONCE OUT OF SIGHT, HE TIED THE END OF THE THREAD TO A ROCK SPUR AND DROPPED THE BALL TO THE GROUND.
OFF YOU GO...

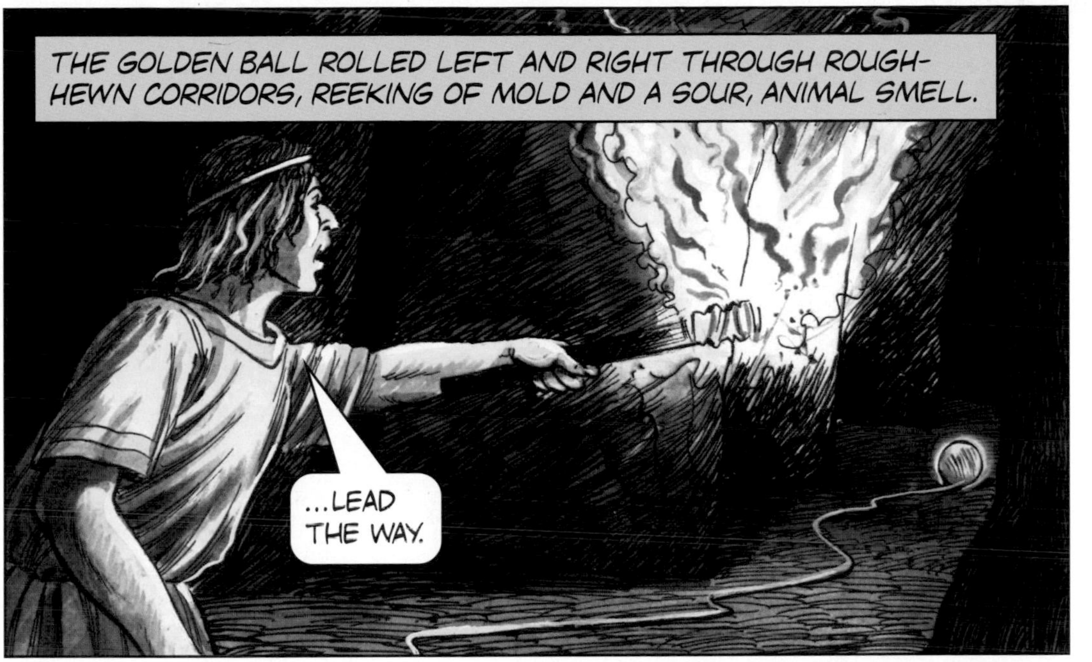
THE GOLDEN BALL ROLLED LEFT AND RIGHT THROUGH ROUGH-HEWN CORRIDORS, REEKING OF MOLD AND A SOUR, ANIMAL SMELL.
...LEAD THE WAY.

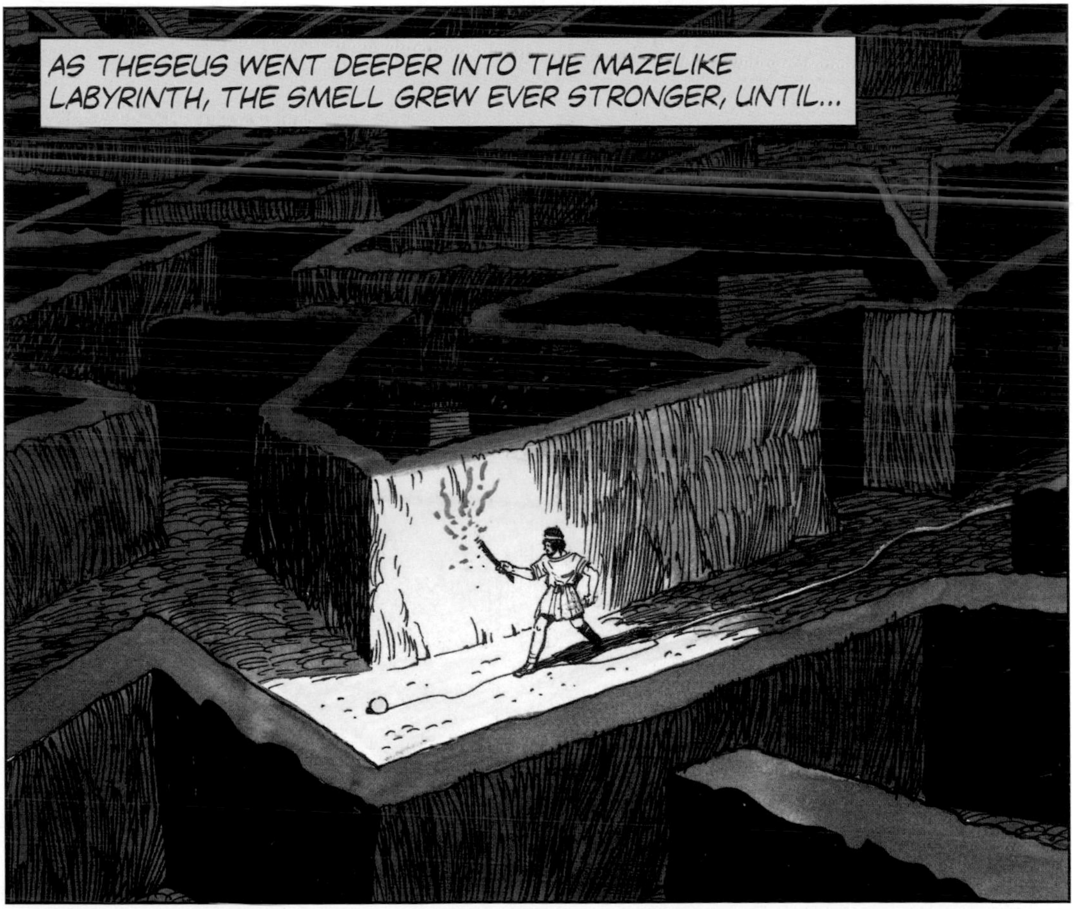
AS THESEUS WENT DEEPER INTO THE MAZELIKE LABYRINTH, THE SMELL GREW EVER STRONGER, UNTIL...

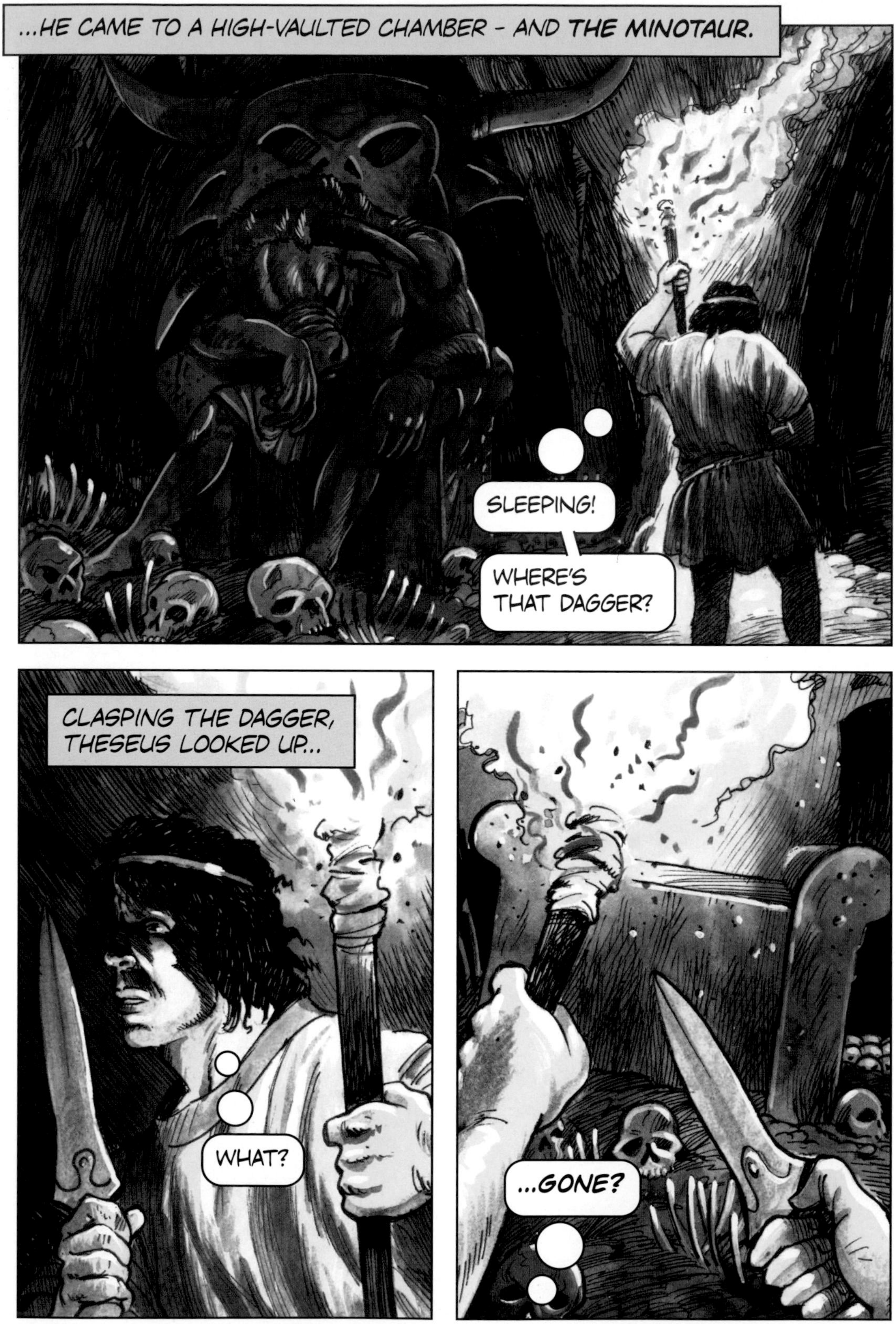
...HE CAME TO A HIGH-VAULTED CHAMBER - AND THE MINOTAUR.
SLEEPING!
WHERE'S THAT DAGGER?
CLASPING THE DAGGER, THESEUS LOOKED UP...
WHAT?
...GONE?

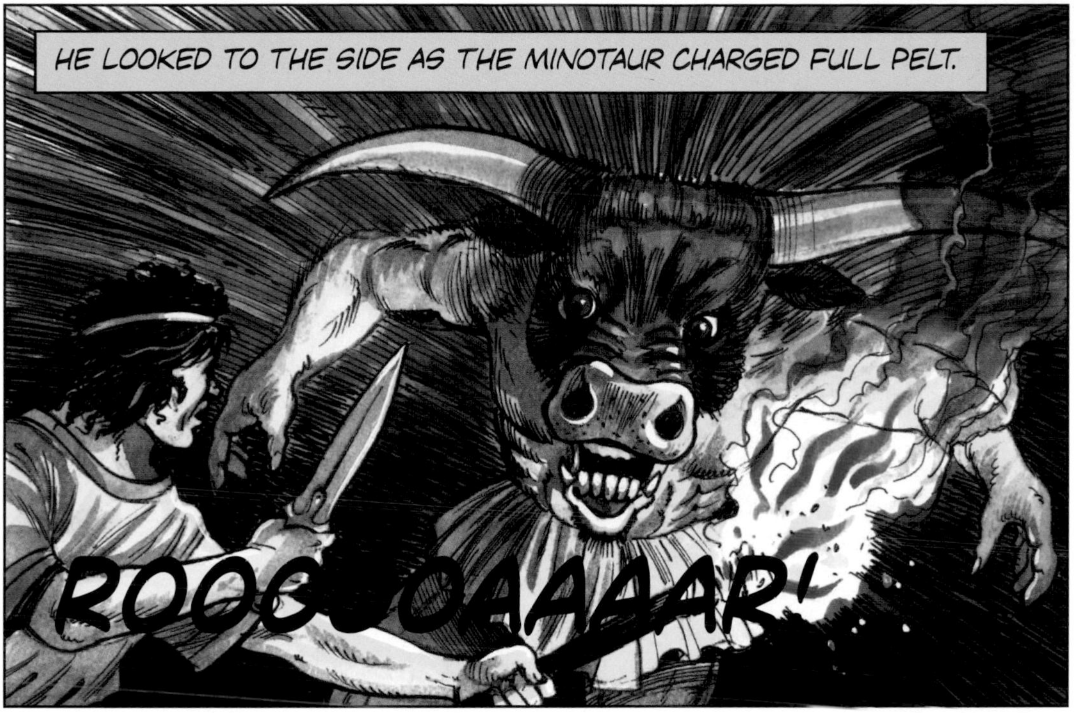
HE LOOKED TO THE SIDE AS THE MINOTAUR CHARGED FULL PELT.

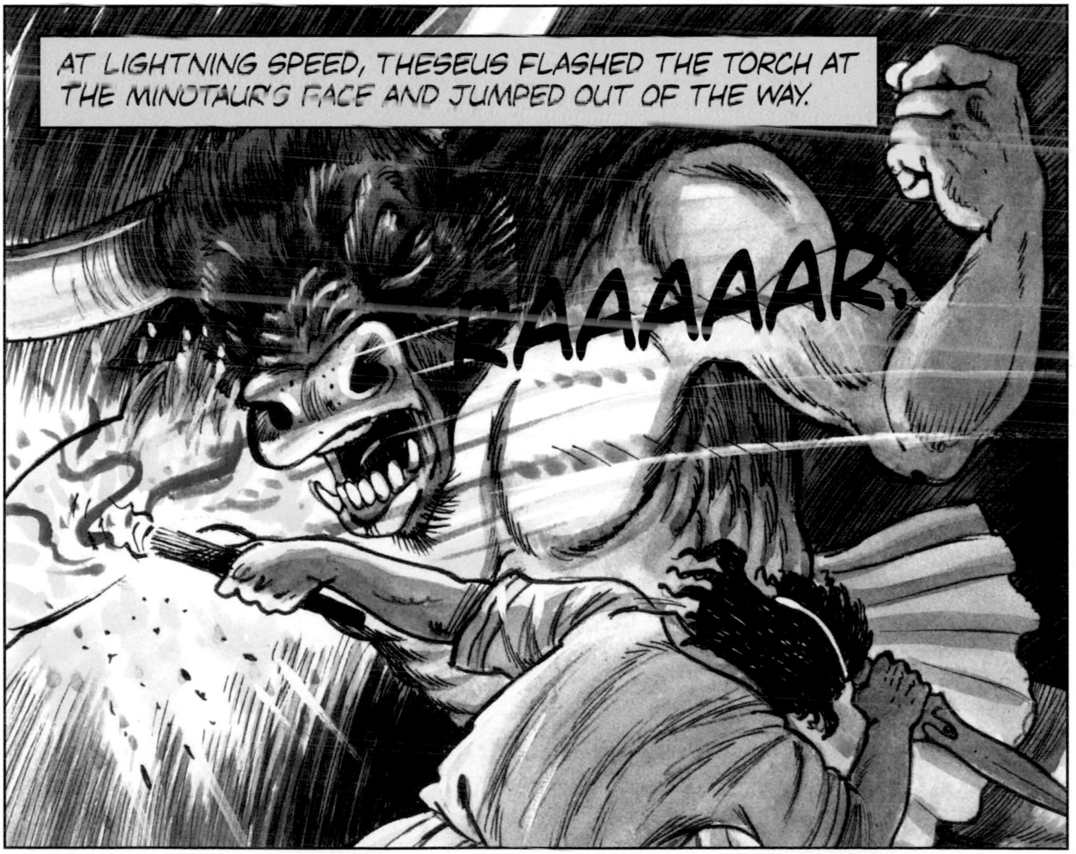
AT LIGHTNING SPEED, THESEUS FLASHED THE TORCH AT THE MINOTAUR'S FACE AND JUMPED OUT OF THE WAY.
RAAAAAR.

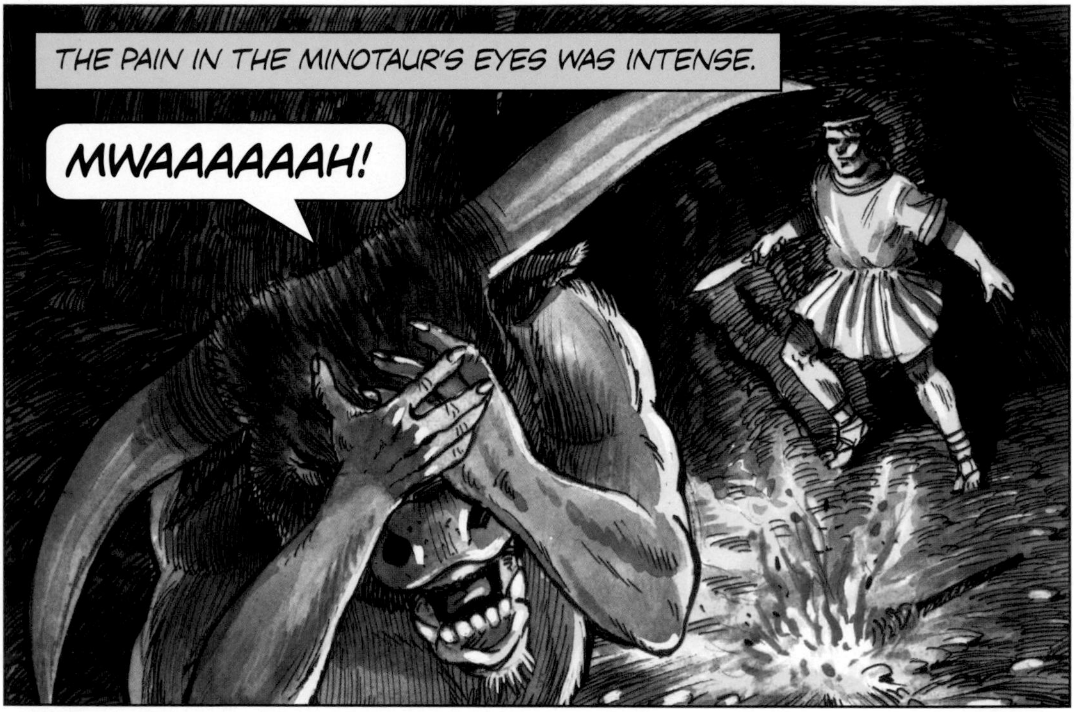
THE PAIN IN THE MINOTAUR'S EYES WAS INTENSE.
MWAAAAAAH!

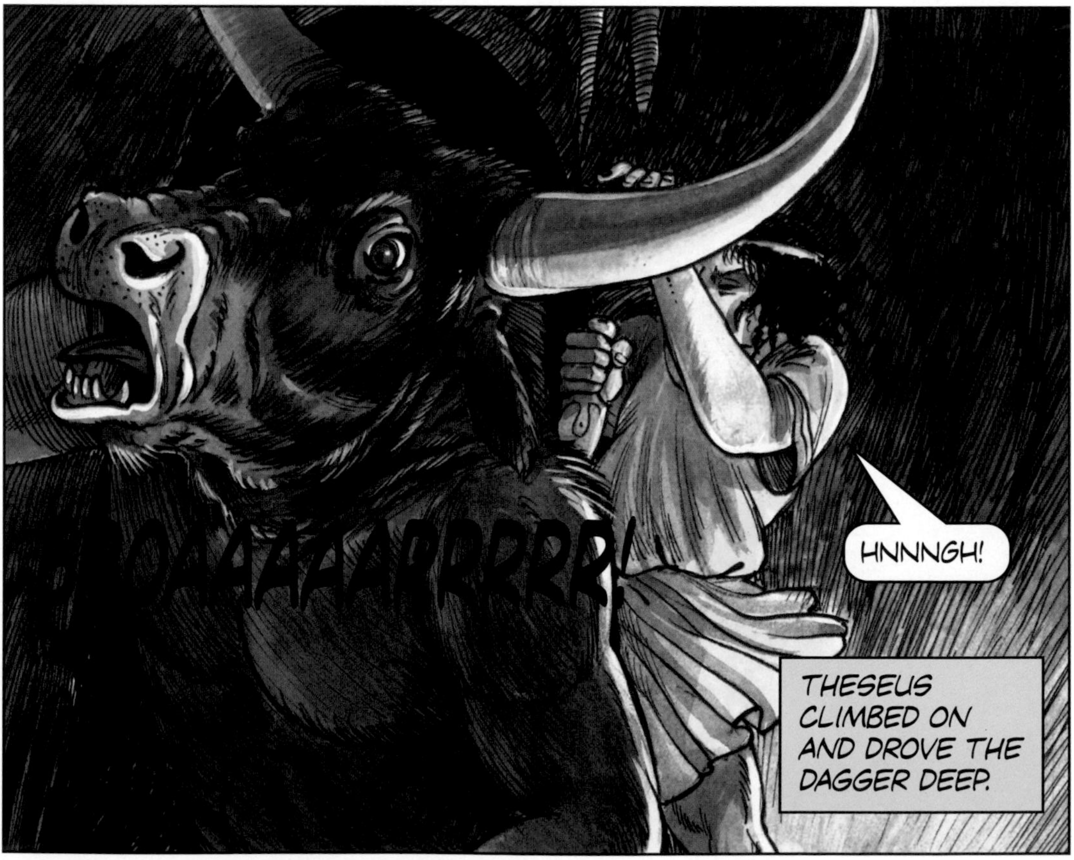
HNNNGH!
THESEUS CLIMBED ON AND DROVE THE DAGGER DEEP.

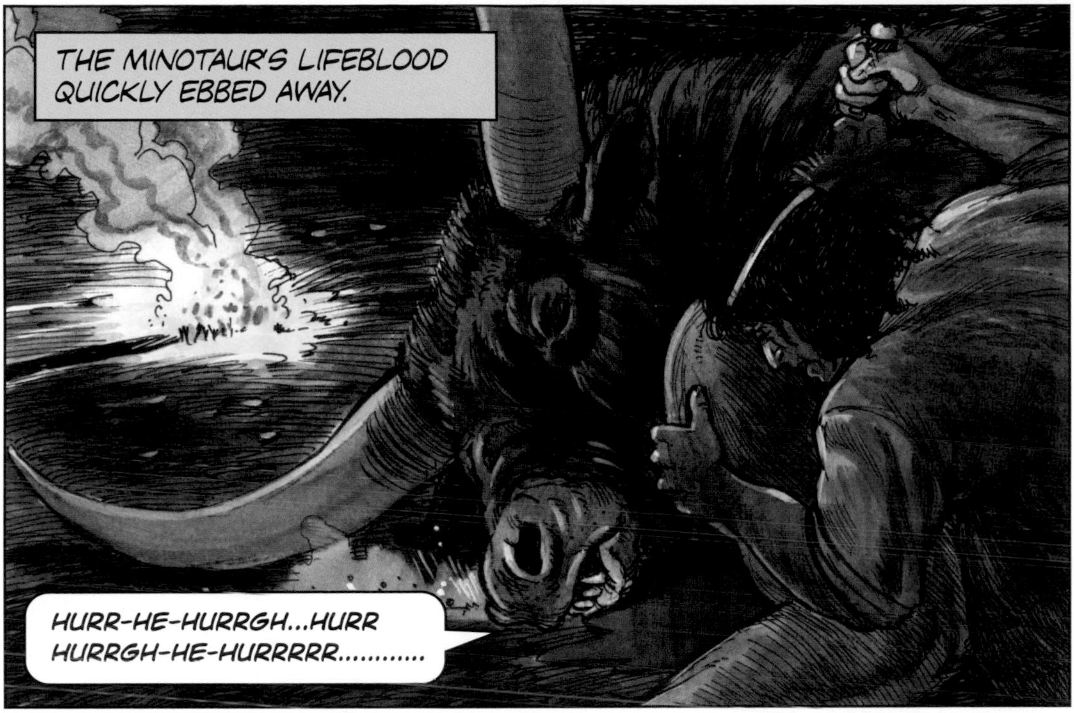
THE MINOTAUR'S LIFEBLOOD QUICKLY EBBED AWAY.
HURR-HE-HURRGH...HURR HURRGH-HE-HURRRRR............

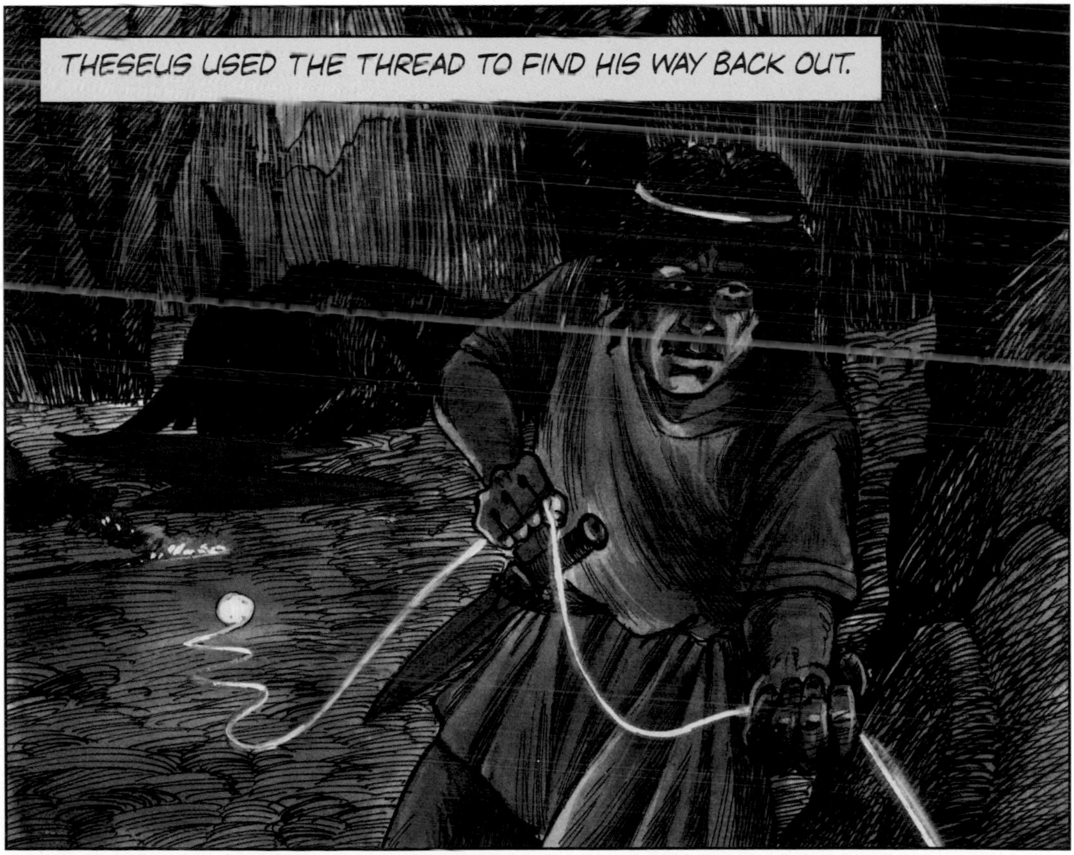
THESEUS USED THE THREAD TO FIND HIS WAY BACK OUT.

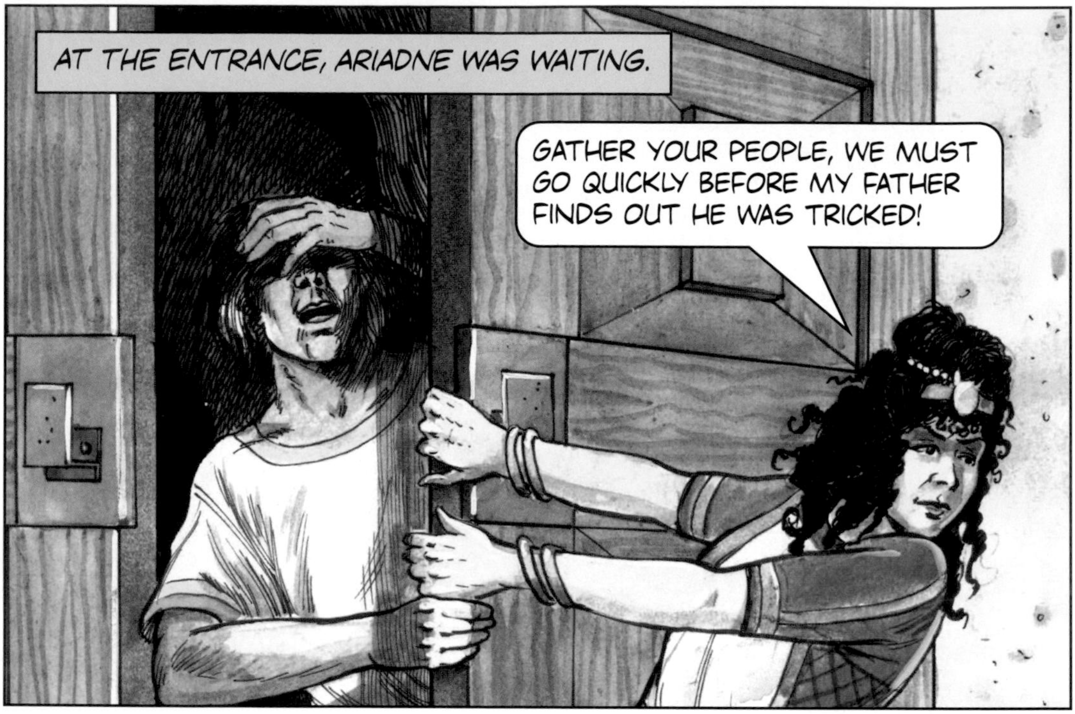
AT THE ENTRANCE, ARIADNE WAS WAITING.
GATHER YOUR PEOPLE, WE MUST GO QUICKLY BEFORE MY FATHER FINDS OUT HE WAS TRICKED!

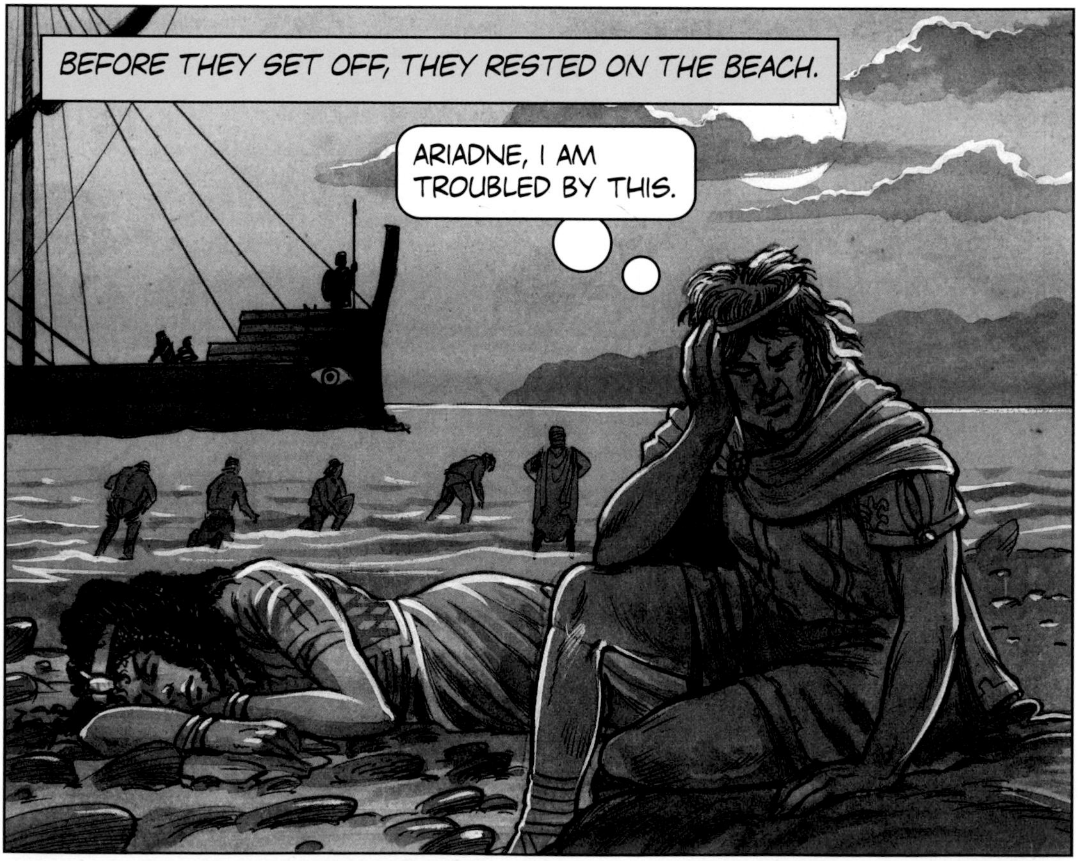
BEFORE THEY SET OFF, THEY RESTED ON THE BEACH.
ARIADNE, I AM TROUBLED BY THIS.

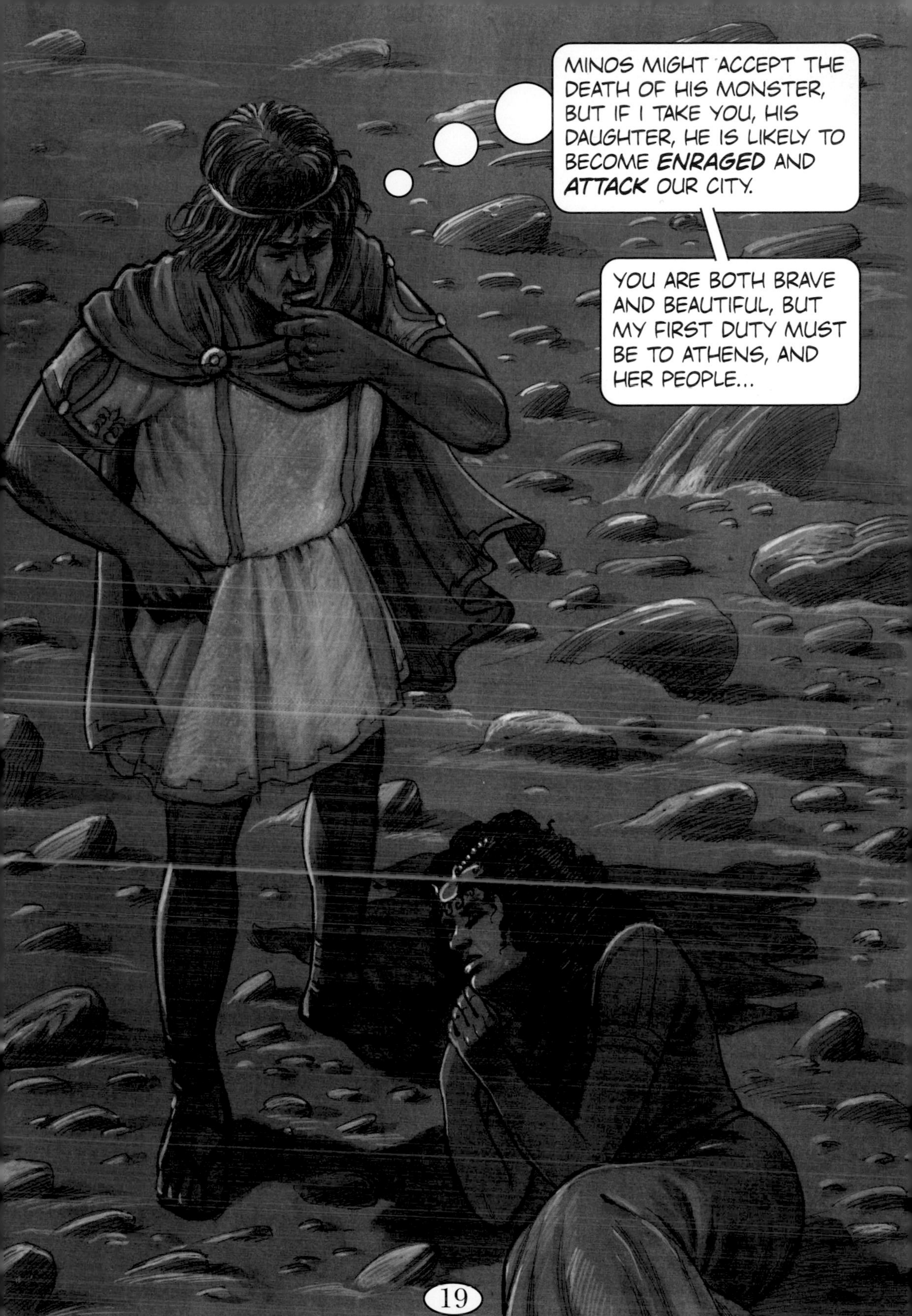
MINOS MIGHT ACCEPT THE DEATH OF HIS MONSTER, BUT IF I TAKE YOU, HIS DAUGHTER, HE IS LIKELY TO BECOME **ENRAGED** AND **ATTACK** OUR CITY.
YOU ARE BOTH BRAVE AND BEAUTIFUL, BUT MY FIRST DUTY MUST BE TO ATHENS, AND HER PEOPLE...

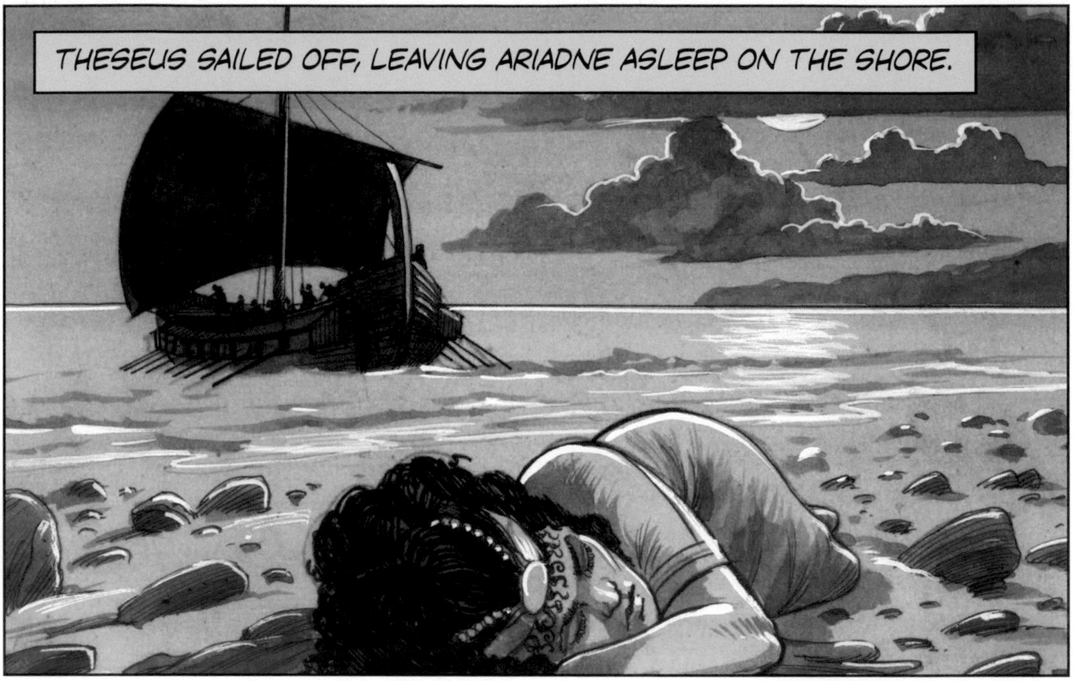
THESEUS SAILED OFF, LEAVING ARIADNE ASLEEP ON THE SHORE.

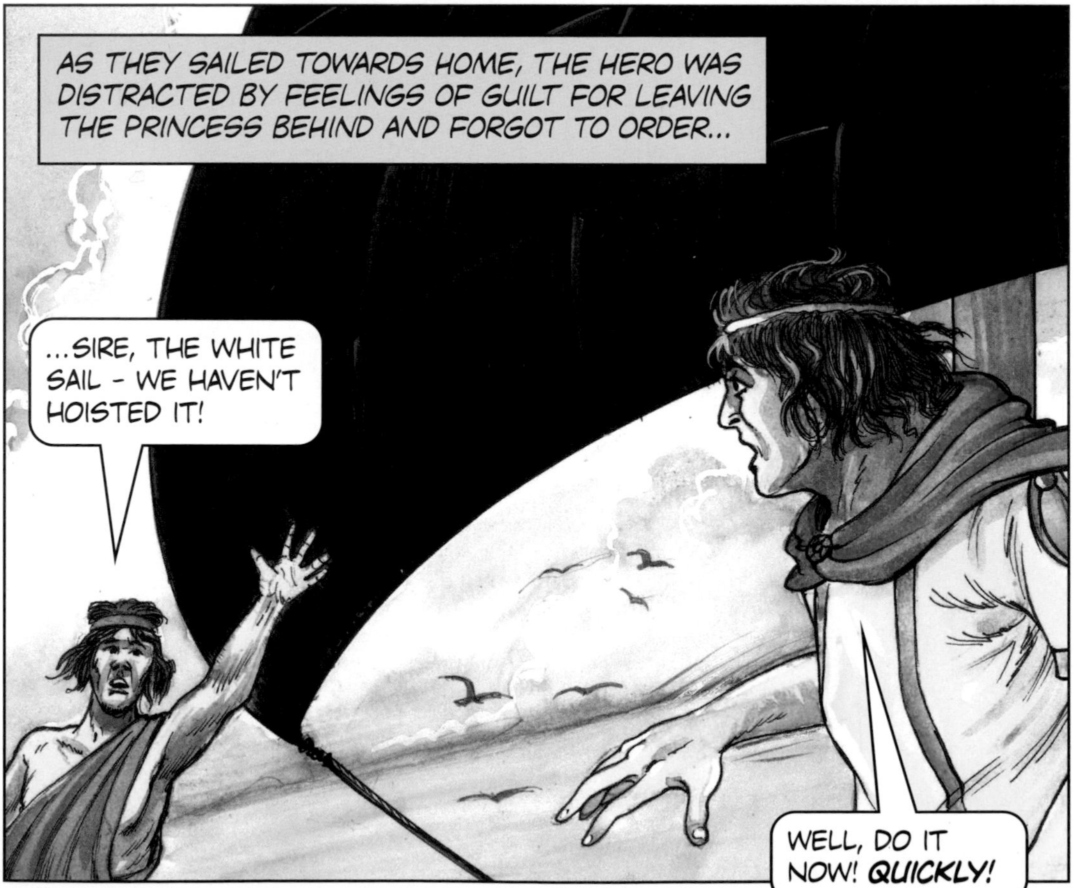
AS THEY SAILED TOWARDS HOME, THE HERO WAS DISTRACTED BY FEELINGS OF GUILT FOR LEAVING THE PRINCESS BEHIND AND FORGOT TO ORDER...
...SIRE, THE WHITE SAIL - WE HAVEN'T HOISTED IT!
WELL, DO IT NOW! **QUICKLY!**

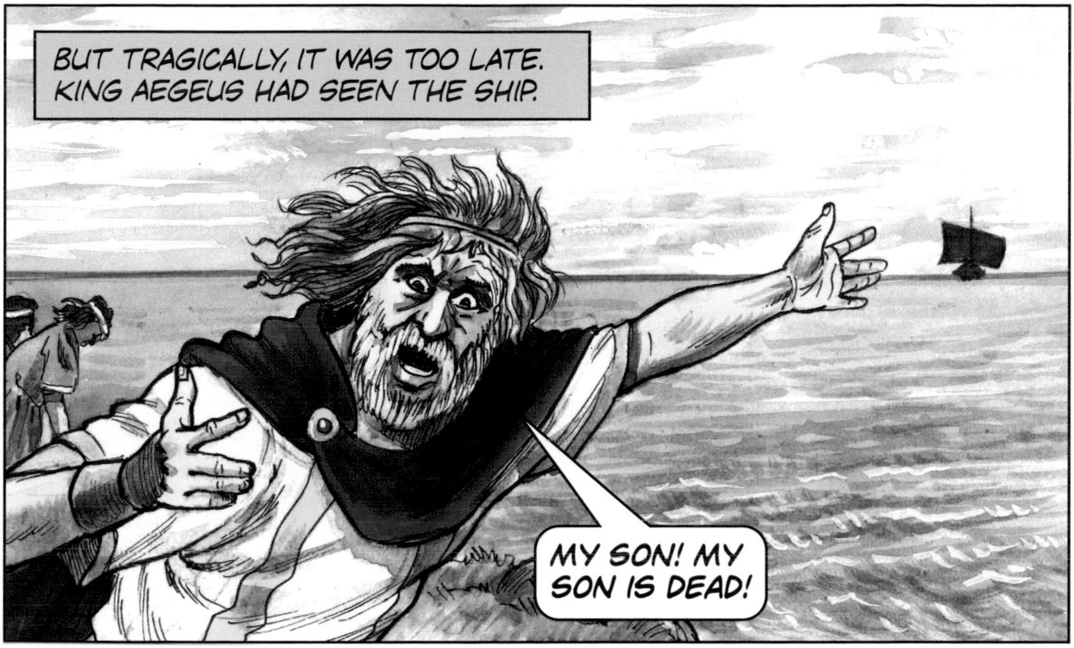
BUT TRAGICALLY, IT WAS TOO LATE. KING AEGEUS HAD SEEN THE SHIP.
MY SON! MY SON IS DEAD!

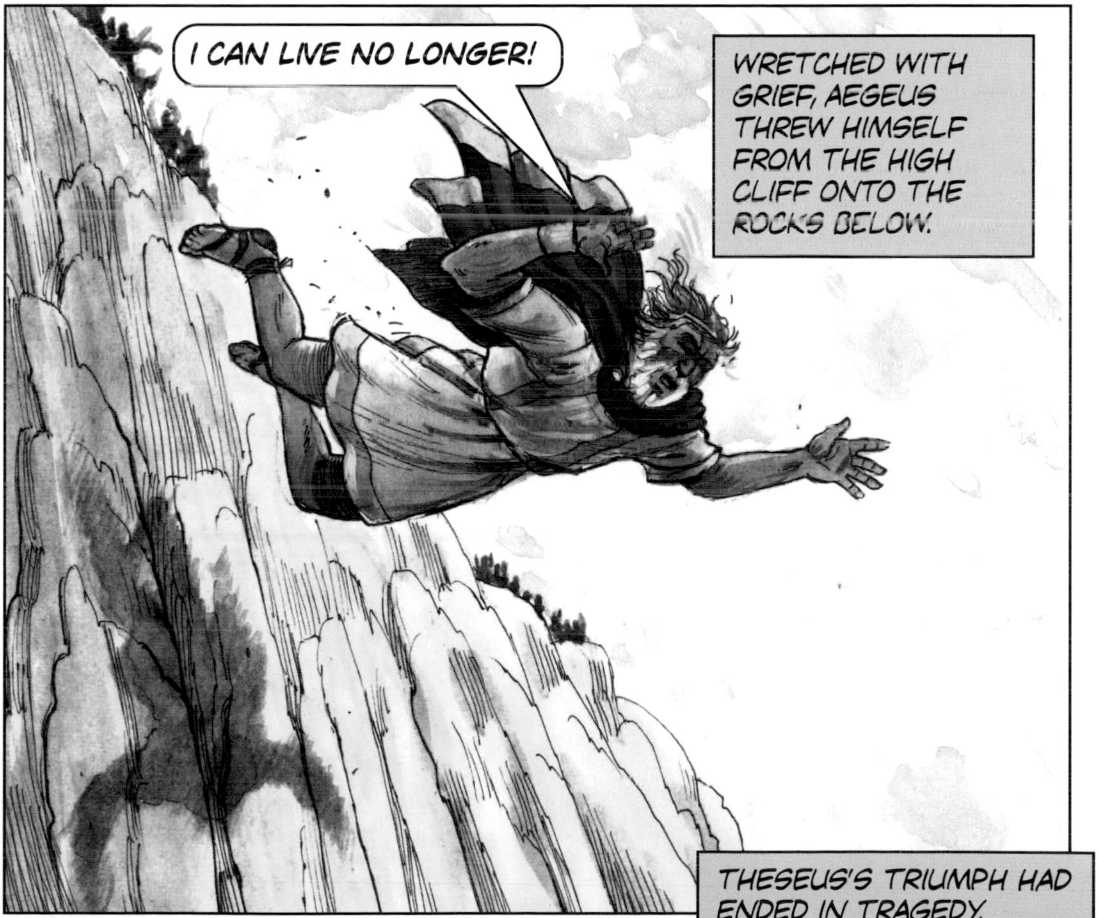
I CAN LIVE NO LONGER!
WRETCHED WITH GRIEF, AEGEUS THREW HIMSELF FROM THE HIGH CLIFF ONTO THE ROCKS BELOW.
THESEUS'S TRIUMPH HAD ENDED IN TRAGEDY.

A Hero's Life

The death of Aegeus meant that Theseus was now king, and the ocean that bordered their lands was named in his father's honor—the Aegean. Dionysus, the god of wine, heard Ariadne sobbing in distress and came down to marry her. Theseus became a celebrated king of Athens.

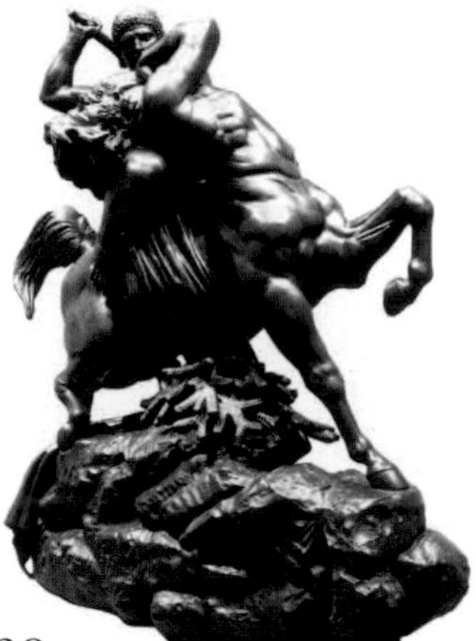

Theseus battles a centaur.

Theseus and Pirithous

Pirithous, king of the Lapiths of Thessaly, heard of Theseus's fame and challenged him by stealing his cattle at Marathon. When Theseus caught up with him, instead of trading blows, they became friends. At the wedding ceremony of Pirithous and Hippodamia, Theseus helped the Lapiths defeat centaurs who had become rowdy on wine.

Theseus in Hades

With his marriage to Hippodamia in doubt, Pirithous decided to marry a goddess instead. He chose Persephone, the wife of Hades and queen of the underworld. Theseus agreed to accompany Pirithous on the dangerous journey to Hades. At the gate, they were met by Hades himself, who offered them a seat. As soon as they sat down, they became rooted to the stone bench. Weeks passed until Hercules appeared and freed Theseus, but Pirithous remained trapped forever.

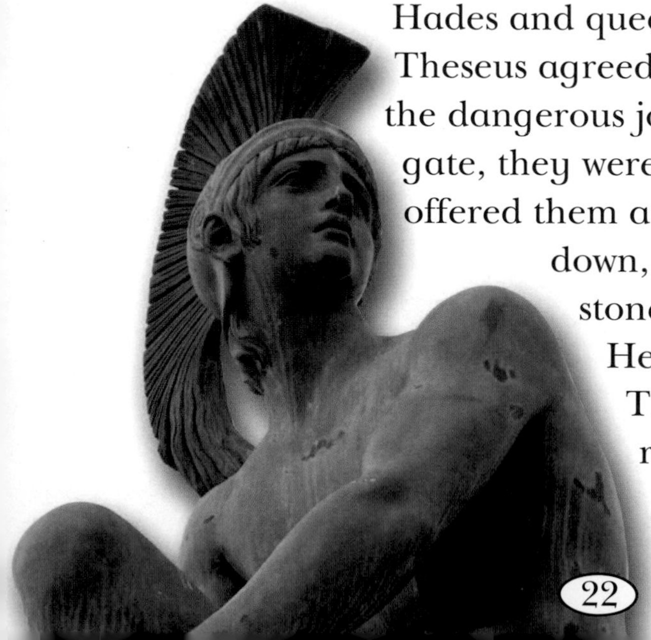

Later, Theseus lost favor with the Athenians and became an outcast.

GLOSSARY

deluded Out of touch with reality.

ebbed Lessened or faded away.

heir The person next in line to become king.

infested Overrun with something unpleasant.

labryinth An underground maze made up of many confusing passageways and dead ends.

Minotaur A hideous mythical beast that is half man and half bull.

notorious Well-known.

reeking Marked by a strong, unpleasant smell.

rough-hewn Uneven and with jagged edges.

rowdy Behaving in an overly enthusiastic, disorderly or loud manner.

sacrifice An offering made to please a god or ruler, often an animal that is killed.

tribute Money or goods given to a ruler as a sign of loyalty and honor.

INDEX